I0162920

The Reason Why I Sing

A Book of Lyrical Songs

By
E.A. James

FM Publishing Company
Cherokee, NC 28719

The Reason Why I Sing
A Book of Lyrical Songs

Published by:

FM Publishing Company
P.O. Box 215
Cherokee, NC 28719
United States of America
www.fmpublishingcompany.com

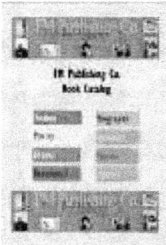

Unless otherwise indicated, all Scripture quotations are taken from The New King James Version. Copyright ©1982, Thomas Nelson, Inc. Publishers. Used by permission.

Copyright © 2010 by E.A. James. All rights reserved. No part of this publication may be reproduced, stored in a retrieval system, or transmitted by any means – electronic, mechanical, photographic (photocopy), recording, or otherwise – without written permission from the publisher.

Printed in the United States of America

ISBN 9781931671118

Library of Congress Control Number 2010936838

Make a joyful noise unto the Lord, all ye lands. Serve the Lord with gladness: come before his presence with singing. Know ye that the Lord he is God: it is he that hath made us, and not we ourselves; we are his people, and the sheep of his pasture. Enter into his gates with thanksgiving, into his courts with praise: be thankful unto him, and bless his name. For the Lord is good; his mercy is everlasting; and his truth endureth to all generations.

Psalm 100

Introduction

Through our powerful prayers we are able to commune with the Most Holy One of Hosts and with His heavenly angels. It delights the soul, renews the spirit, and enlightens the mind. This collection of songs was borne out of those prayers and heartfelt communion with His Majesty.

These songs span a period of 33 years from 1987 to 2010. They represent my spiritual search, spiritual conversion, and experiences with various churches, pastors, and believers. They are a collection of my praise and worship from the still quiet whispers with tears and thanksgiving — to the loud, tongue-speaking, hand-clapping and feet-stomping *shabach* times with Jesus.

Although I can always hear the music in my head, unlike Mozart, I am not adept at scoring. Therefore, I have recorded the lyrics only. These are my Book of Psalms (Songs). Just as the Bible's Psalms have been recorded without the music scores, whereby each individual singer (believer) can allow the music of their own salvation to "sing" the psalm within them, so too my Book of Songs allows each believer to create his or her own music, beat, and tempo to manifest one's own harmonious walk in the Spirit.

Use them in your devotion times. Use them in your worship — whether individually or when assembled with other believers. In so doing, you too will discover and be able to tell anyone who asks, *The Reason Why I Sing*.

Table of Contents

Table of Contents (cont'd)

6

Stand Fast

Stand fast and see God's glory

Stand fast
And see Him reign
Stand fast
And look to Jesus
Stand fast
For He's coming again

He took me up
And showed me a better place
He said I'll be with you
And I'll help you to run this race

So, stand fast

There's No One like Jesus

With this pen I write
To tell of the Savior
No one in this world
Can liken unto His majesty

Look to Jesus for salvation
He shed His blood on a tree
Heed His words He speaks to you
There's no one like Him

Put your trust in His hands
They took the nails for you
Always abound in His love
There's no one like Jesus

As red as the ink is upon this page
His blood poured forth
So that we might live eternally
There's no one like Jesus

You might think it strange
To glorify what we haven't seen
But His love and sacrifice
Is all the proof I need

There's No One like Jesus (cont'd)

When I should die

Please remember His love in me

The light is a dark place

There's no one like Jesus

Prayer of Israel

Forgive me, Lord
Heal me, Lord
Hear me, Lord
Save me, Lord in Jesus' Name

Teach me, Lord
Show me, Lord
Speak to me, Lord
Fill me, Lord in Jesus Name

Walk with me, Lord
Talk with me, Lord
Lead me, Lord
Use me, Lord in Jesus Name

Help me, Lord
Keep me, Lord
Thank you, Lord
I love you, Lord in Jesus Name

Amen.

Psalm 40:1

I need your Spirit in me
I need you Lord to make me free
Oh, nothing can save me now but you
I finally know it Lord it's true

Oh, Pick me up and set my feet,
Plant them Lord on solid ground
I know you'll never leave me Lord
You said I'll always be around

Help me Lord to make it through
And tell me Lord just what to do
I place my life within your hands
Show me Jesus, all your plans

Give me patience, peace, and love
Born of wings of the heavenly dove
So I can wait to know your will
And you to say, "Peace be still"

Soul is Saved, Satisfied

Verse 1: No more worries
No more fears
Troubles may come
And they may bring tears
But I've got Jesus on my side
He's my Savior and I'm His bride

Chorus: Soul is saved, satisfied
Soul is saved, satisfied
Soul is saved, satisfied
My soul is saved
And I'm satisfied

Verse 2: I've got that oil
To carry me through
The Holy Ghost power
That makes me new
He washed my sins and fears away
Love shines through
So I'm here to say

Chorus
(Repeat from Verse 2)

Author and Finisher of My Faith

Choir: Jesus is the author and finisher of my faith
(Repeat 4 xs)

He who has begun a good work in you
Trust in Him and He will see it through

Believe in His saving grace until the end
Though all forsake you He'll be your friend

Jesus is the author and finisher of my faith
(Repeat)

I'm baptized with His blood in His name
Old man's crucified, I'm not the same

Holy Ghost power cam on me
Praise His name 'cause now I'm set free

Choir: Jesus is the author and finisher of my faith
(Repeat 4 xs)

Sopranos: Author and Finisher
Author and Finisher of my faith
(Repeat)

Author and Finisher of My Faith (cont'd)

Altos & Tenors: Author of my Faith
Finisher of my Faith
Author of my Faith
Finisher of my Faith
(Repeat)

Choir: Jesus is the author and finisher of my faith
(Repeat 4 xs)

He who has begun
He who has begun
A good work in you

He will see it through
He will see it through
A good work in you
(Repeat)

Author of my Faith
Finisher of my Faith
(Repeat 3 times)

Psalm 98

O sing unto the Lord a new song
For He has done marvelous things
-O sing unto the Lord a new song
And you'll see the joy that it brings

O He has made know his salvation
His righteousness is open to sight
O praise Him with joyful elation
And others will see His great light

Refrain: Rejoice, now, sing praises
Make a joyful noise all the earth
Rejoice, now, sing praise
For victory comes through rebirth

Let the trumpet sound
Let the haps rejoice
Sound the comet (or cornet) to Him
Let the earth hear your voice

And the son will roar
And the floods clap their hands
For the Lord, He will judge
All people and lands

No One like Jesus

Chorus: There is no one
     No one like Jesus
     No one like Jesus
     No one like my Jesus
He can be the Father
He can be the Son
When the Holy Ghost comes upon you
You'll know Messiah is the one

I feel Him in my soul
Can't you hear my spirit moan
Oh, precious Jesus
Come and take me home

Chorus

I believe He was
I believe that He is
I believe He shall be
For every eye to see

He's coming back
Coming back for me
Shout Hallelujah
Praise the Lord! Victory!

John 14:1-6

I will come again
I will come some day
I will come again, my child
So watch, be ready, and pray

Let not your heart be troubled
Neither let it be afraid
In my Father's House are many mansions
And a place for you I have laid

For I go to prepare a place for you
And I will come again
So that where I am you may be
For I call you more than friend

Where I go, my child, you know
And yes, you know the way
For I am the way, the truth, the life
My blood, has left no sin to pay

So my peace I leave with you
But not as the world might give
I leave the Holy Ghost in you
My child so you might live

Born Again

Chorus: You must be born again
You must be born again
You must be born again
My friend
(Repeat)

Lead: Will you be with us
When the Lord comes again
When He comes
Will you be there?

Our lives are but a whisper
One day you're here and then you're gone
But you can live a holy life
When you make Jesus your number one

Chorus: You must be born again
You must be born again
You must be born again
My friend
(Repeat)

Born Again (cont'd)

Lead: I know it seems so strange
The things that I talk about
But if you listen to His Spirit
In your heart there won't be a doubt

Won't you come to Him today?
He'll save your soul in a special way
Just tell Him God, forgive my sin
Yes God, I want to be born again

Chorus: You must be born again
You must be born again
You must be born again
My friend

When I Feel His Spirit

(1) *Chorus:* I feel the Spirit
I feel it move
When I feel the Spirit
My Soul can't refuse

It moves deep within me
I feel it coming out
When I feel the Spirit
I can't help but jump and shout
(Repeat Chorus)

(2) **Change**: Move inside, move inside
Move inside of me
(Repeat)

(3) **Sopranos**: Move inside of me (4 x's)

Altos: Move inside, move inside
Move inside of me
(Repeat)

Tenors: Move, Spirit, Move (4 x's)

(4) All voices simultaneously--their respective parts!

(5) **Change**: Back to (1)

When I Feel His Spirit (cont'd)

(6) *Chorus*: I feel the Spirit (4 x's)

Can <u>you</u> feel the Spirit? (4 x's)

(7) **S & A's:** Brothers, can you feel the Spirit?

Tenors: Yes, we can feel the Spirit!

Sisters, can you feel the Spirit!

S & A's: Yes, we can feel the Spirit!

Speak Through Me

Chorus: Speak through me, Lord
Speak through me, Lord
Speak through me, Lord
Speak through me, Lord (repeat)

I know you love me, Lord
And you always have
Thanks for helping me to see
Thanks Lord, for eye salve

I want to tell them all about you
I want them to know your name
Speak the words so they can hear
Before you come again

Chorus
Jesus died on a tree
He came to save your soul
He rose again that third day
So He could take control

You need to repent of all your sins
So He can take you in
He's waiting for you with open arms
Your heart He wants to win

Speak Through Me (cont'd)

Chorus

1. **Sopranos**: Speak through me, Lord

    Speak through me, Lord

    Speak through me, Lord

    Speak through me, Lord

All put together (4 x's - after Tenors come in do their part)

    Speak through me – Lord!

2. **Altos**: (come in) Speak through me, Lord

3. **Tenors**: (come in) Speak through me, Lord

    (4 x's)

    Speak through me, Lord

Nothing but the Truth

Lead: Matthew tell us the story
The same one you told the Hebrews
Who rebelled and would not listen
When you tried to share the news

That Jesus is the true Messiah
Messiah he is and King of Kings
Even one other King named Martin
Knew through Jesus freedom rings

Chorus: Nothing But the Truth so help me God
Nothing But the Truth so help me God
Nothing, nothing, nothing but The Truth
Oh, nothing but The Truth so help me God
(Repeat)

Lead: Mark was the first to testify
To the believers who lived in Rome
Of Jesus, a servant on the move
Travelling miles from His home

Healing the sick and feeding the poor
Accepting all who would come
He taught and worked many miracles
So that countless souls were won

Nothing but the Truth (cont'd)

Chorus *(repeat 2 xs)*

Lead: Luke gave us details, an accurate account
Of the salvation that Jesus gives
Born of a virgin and the Holy Spirit
The perfect man, our Savior lives

Baptized of "one crying in the wilderness"
One unworthy to unlatch his shoes
Who knew he must decrease while He increase
As a dove signified who God would use

Chorus

Lead: John testified in the beginning was the word
And the same was with God and was God
Jesus, Holy Master of all creation,
Preached repentance wherever He trod

Saying, "I am the Light of the world"
The Life, the Way, the Truth, the Gate
Cease from sin and keep His commandments
Watch, be ready, take heed, and wait!

Chorus: Nothing but The Truth so help me God
Nothing but The Truth so help me God
Nothing, nothing, nothing, but The Truth
Oh, nothing but The Truth so help me God
(Repeat)

Just give me The Truth (so help me God)
And nothing but The Truth (nothing else, God)
(Repeat)

Just give me The Truth, God (softly)
(Repeat 3 times)

Just give me The Truth, God (loudly)
(Repeat 3 times)

Just give me The Truth! (Hold high note)

God's Answer

In My Name
I cleanse your sins
And will change old to new
I heal your infirmities
And all that wars within you
I hear your prayer and ask
That you be born again
My blood shall cover you
From this day forth
And protect you to the end.

In My Name
I give you my word--old and new
All of it surely testifies
They are examples and ensamples
Of things to come--
Assuring my word never dies
Test every spirit when
I make known my will
As a sign, you will speak
With other tongues
As the Holy Spirit's power
Does fill.

God's Answer (cont'd)

In My Name
I am with you always
And will direct your path
Do all that is pleasing
To forsake my wrath
I seek a vessel
That is tried in the fire
One who'll work with a
Diligent heart
That is the vessel which I desire
A clean, pure, and holy temple
Is where I reside--
One, obedient and faithful--
Not even a jot or a tittle to hide

In My Name
Know that before you ask
Deliverance is on its way
And I chasten my sheep
When they willfully go astray
Your needs are not great
That I cannot fulfill
Know that I AM GOD
And all ye waiting hearts
BE STILL.

I Will Call Your Name

In the morning, Yes Lord
In the morning, Yes Lord
In the afternoon, Yes Lord
I will call your name
I will call your name
I will call your name
Yes Lord (repeat)

Yes Lord, Yes Lord
Yes Lord, Yes Lord
I will call your name

In the morning, Yes Lord
In the morning, Yes Lord
I will call your name

I will call your name
In the afternoon
I will call your name
In the afternoon
I will call your name

I will call your name (soprano)
I will call your name (alto)
I will call your name (tenor)
I will call your name (all & hold)

I Will Call Your Name (cont'd)

Father, Father, I will call your name
Messiah Jesus, I will call your name
Holy Spirit, I will call your name
I will call your name

Lord, Lift Me Up

Lord, lift me up

Lord, fill my cup

Lord, lift me up

Lord, fill my cup

Lord, lift me higher

Higher than I've ever been

Lord, fill me up

Fill me, Lord

Once again

What I Can Do

I'm standing for you
I'm standing for you
I'm standing for you
I'm standing for you
Standing, standing, standing for you
I'm praying for you
I'm praying for you
I'm praying for you
I'm praying for you
Praying, praying, praying for you
But I can't live for you
I can't live for you
I can't live for you
I can't live for you
That is something you must do

Anoint Me, Lord

Anointing, fall on me

Anointing, fall on me

Lord, let your Spirit fall on me

Anointing, fall on me

Anointing, fall on us

Anointing, fall on us

Lord, let your Spirit fall on us

Anointing, fall on us

Anointing, cleanse my soul

Anointing, cleanse my soul

Lord, let your Spirit cleanse my soul

Anointing, cleanse my soul

Anointing, purge my sins

Anointing, purge my sins

Lord, let your Spirit purge my sins

Anointing, purge my sins

Anointing, work in me

Anointing, work in me

Lord, let your Spirit work in me

Anointing, work in me

Anointing, show me my call

Anointing, show me my call

Lord, let your Spirit show me my call

Anointing, show me my call

Move On In Faith

Unite us Lord and bind us as one
Oh Lord, we've only begun
We've been rooted and grounded and shown how
There's no stopping us now
We're going to move on, move on, move on in faith
Move on in faith

Open To Jesus

Open my eyes, Lord
I want to see Jesus
Open my eyes, Lord
I want to see Him
Open to my ears, Lord
So I can hear your voice
Open my lips, Lord
So I can rejoice
Open my heart, Lord
And teach me to love
Open my mind, Lord
To your knowledge above

Jesus, My Everything

Today I saw somebody who looked just like you
Lord, he talked like you too, so I thought it was you
But as I searched the scriptures down on my knees
Begging you please, Lord show me the truth
I need your truth
Now I know you Lord, I know for myself
And there is no one else who can lead me astray
Not this day
You are everything,
Jesus everything is you in my life
You are everything, Jesus everything is you
You're everything, everything, everything to me
I am just convinced that you Lord are real
Because your Spirit I feel and He lives in me, yes in me
And I'm no longer shy and I can boldly say
That now I am saved in the gospel way
You are everything,
Jesus everything is you in my life
You are everything, Jesus everything is you
You're everything, everything, everything to me
I love you Lord, with all of my heart,
My soul and my mind
And with all of my strength

Jesus, My Everything (cont'd)

And when I hear your voice, I have no choice
But to follow you for the rest of my days
You are everything,
Jesus everything is you in my life
You are everything, Jesus everything is you
You're everything, everything, everything to me

It's in Your Hands, Lord

Healing is in your hands
Healing is in thy hands
Healing is in thy hands, oh Lord, it's in your hands
Love is in thy hands
Love is in thy hands
Love is in thy hands;
Peace is in thy hands
Peace is in thy hands
Peace is in thy hands;
Joy is in thy hands
Joy is in thy hands
Joy is in thy hands;
Jesus, it's in thy hands
Jesus, it's in thy hands
Jesus, it's in thy hands;

Here I Am, Send Me

God looked and He said

My harvest is plentiful

Yea, I need laborers

Oh, I need those who will do my will

And I said God, Oh God

Here I am, Oh, here I am

Here I am, send me

So the Spirit of The Lord is upon me

Because He has anointed me

To preach good tidings, oh, oh

unto the meek

He sent me, oh yes, He has sent me

To bind the broken-hearted

And to proclaim liberty

To the captives to the captives in sin

He has sent me to open the doors of freedom

To them, to them, to them, that are bound

He has sent me

He has sent me

He has sent me

And not myself

Cause I wanted to worship Him

And I wanted to please Him

And I wanted to do His will

Here I Am, Send Me (cont'd)

So I said God

Here I am

Here I am

Here I am

Send me

Here I am, Lord

Here I am, Lord

Here I am

Send me

Jesus Lifted Me Up

Jesus lifted me up
When I was falling down
Then He changed my life
Totally turned it upside down
He said this is the way
My child, so walk herein
And I will be with you
I'll be with you till the end
So, come on, praise His name
He's worthy to be praised
Come on, praise His name
Yes, He's worthy to be praised

Nothing Can Keep God from Me

Ain't no mountain high enough
Ain't no river wide enough
Ain't no valley low enough
To keep God from me
(repeat)
Just call His name and you don't have to worry
Just call His name, He'll be there in a hurry
Just say Jesus, and He's right there
Just say Jesus, and He's right there
Say wash me Lord, clean me through and through
Wash me Lord, I want to be just like you
Cause there ain't no mountain high enough
Ain't no river wide enough
Ain't no valley low enough
To keep God from you
And there ain't no mountain high enough
Ain't no river wide enough
Ain't no valley low enough
To keep God from me
I just call His name, and I don't have to worry
I just call His name, and he's there in a hurry
I say Jesus, and He's right there
I say Jesus, and He's right there

Nothing Can Keep God from Me (cont'd)

Cause there ain't no mountain high enough

Ain't no river wide enough

Ain't no valley low enough

To keep God from me

A Wanderer's Theme Song

My heritage, my land
A place to call my own
I don't know why I wandered
I wandered around so long
My heritage, my land
What I needed so desperately
Was obedience to God in Messiah
My allegiance to God in Messiah
Yes, to return to God in Messiah
To live eternally in me

Our Heritage

Our heritage, our home

And we're one big family

And he gave us a gentle shepherd

Who rules with grace and sovereignty

Our heritage, our home

And we're one big family

And we will work together

And we will pray together

So we can worship in unity

God's Kingdom

God's Kingdom, God's home
He made us one big family
With Jesus as our gentle pastor
To unite us in harmony
God's Kingdom, God's home
He rules over our big family
And we make disciples
As we praise His name
And of His mighty word
We're never ashamed
For one day we'll live with Him eternally

Out of the Mouth of Babes

People are people
Whatever they do
Just make sure their faults
Don't become a part of you
Jesus is the answer
For the world today
He'll help you though
If you only learn to pray
Trust in The Lord
With all of your heart
That's when you know
You're truly smart
Jesus is the answer
Jesus is the answer
For the world today
He'll help you though
If you only learn to pray

The Light in the Darkness

Jesus, you're the light in the darkness
You're the warmth in the cold
And you knew me even before I was born
So I know you'll be with me when I'm old
And I will praise your name
I'll praise your name
I will praise your holy name
And I will praise your name
I'll praise you name
I will praise your holy name

Do You Have a Testimony?

Do you have a testimony to tell

Has God fixed you up and made you well

Has He lifted you this day

Has He shown you a better way

Do you have a testimony to tell

Do you have a praise report to give

Has He taught you a better way to live

Has He done something for you

That no one else could do

Do you have a praise report to give

Do you have a testimony to tell

Is it overflowing in you like a well

Then don't just sit there in your seat

Won't you tell us how God's been sweet

Do you have a testimony to tell

Jesus, the Cornerstone

He was rejected of men, rejected of men
For all the eyes to see
And I know how He felt
Because I know how I wept
When they all rejected me
The stone that the builders rejected
Has become the cornerstone
And He makes intercession for you and for me
And He'll never leave us alone
Jesus the Cornerstone
You, Messiah, are my cornerstone
So when men reject you
Just say, Lord I need you
And just hold your head up high
And He'll lift you up
And He'll fill your cup
And He'll help you to get by
The stone that the builders rejected
Has become the cornerstone
And He makes intercession for you and for me
And He'll never leave us alone, Jesus the Cornerstone
You Messiah, are my cornerstone
You Messiah, are my cornerstone
Jesus, the cornerstone

The Lord is my Shepherd

The Lord is my shepherd

I shall not want

I shall not lack any good thing

To Jesus Messiah

I lift my voice

To Him only do I sing

The Lord is the Good Shepherd

And he leads me

He opens my eyes

And finally I see

Whenever I look over my shoulder

To the left I see Goodness

To the right I see Mercy

And I know they are always behind me

For The Lord is my shepherd

I shall not want

I shall not lack any good thing

Move, Spirit, Move

I feel the Holy Spirit
I feel it move
When I feel His Spirit
My soul can't refuse
I feel it coming out
When I feel His Spirit
I can't help but jump and shout
Move, Spirit, move
Move inside of me
Oh, move, Spirit, move
Move inside of me

His Name is Jesus

Chorus: His name is Jesus (3 x's)
Jesus, my Messiah

His name is Justice
His name is Mercy
His name is Everlasting Love, Peace, and Joy

Oh call upon Him
He'll always answer
He's there for every woman, man, girl and boy

Chorus

If you don't know Him
It's time to know Him
Time you went on down in Jesus's name

Tell Satan goodbye
I'm gone forever
I've been free since the Holy Ghost done came

Yahoshua Is My Song

Yah – ho – shua
Yah – ho – shua
To thee I sing; Let freedom ring
Yah – ho – o – shua

Yah – ho – shua
Yah – ho – shua
This time I know and I won't let go
Yah – ho – o – shua

Yah – ho – shua
Yah – ho – shua
You died for me to set me free
Yah – ho – o – shua

Yah – ho – shua
Yah – ho – shua
No more a slave to the ones from the cave
Yah – ho – o – shua

Yah – ho – shua
Yah – ho – shua
I belong to you though one of the few
Yah – ho – o – shua

Yah – ho – shua
Yah – ho – shua
Sing HALLELUYAH! HALLELUYAH
Yah – ho – o – shua!

The Seed of Abraham

Oh create in me a clean heart
A clean heart is what I need
Oh create in me a clean heart
That's the prayer of Abraham's Seed

Our fathers disobeyed you
And for this sin we were cursed
The nations would rule over us
So unto them we were dispersed

Oh create in me a clean heart
A clean heart is what I need
Oh create in me a clean heart
That's the prayer of Abraham's Seed

The prophets came to warn us
To preach judgment from God
But the people would not listen
And the Savior they would slay

Oh create in me a clean heart
A clean heart is what I need
Oh create in me a clean heart
That's the prayer of Abraham's Seed

Oh Father please forgive us
For we know not what we do
There can be no true salvation
Until our hearts turn back to you

Oh create in me a clean heart
A clean heart is what I need
Oh create in me a clean heart
That's the prayer of Abraham's Seed

The Seed of Abraham (Cont'd)

Oh Zion, sing praises
Sing praises once again
For the Father has redeemed us
With his mighty outstretched hand

Oh create in me a clean heart
A clean heart is what I need
Oh create in me a clean heart
That's the prayer of Abraham's Seed

About The Author

Dr. Elizabeth A. James (E.A. James) has been writing for over 40 years. She is a licensed and ordained minister and has been President and Founder of Fast And Indispensable Temporary Help (F.A.I.T.H.) Ministries, Inc. since February, 1999. She is also the Editor-in-Chief of FM Publishing Company (2009) and Senior Managing Director of Geri Lorraine Enterprises, LLC (2000). In 2014, she became a supplier, independent marketer, and supporter with TAG Team Marketing International and a dedicated member of the Black Business Network.

After attending over 10 colleges, she has a doctorate in Theology & Biblical Counseling, a master's in Education, bachelor's degree in English, and major course work in subjects such as Business Management, Biomedical Engineering, Pre-Med, and Chemistry.

In addition to many other accomplishments, E.A. James has received the Woman of Excellence Award, is a member of blackwritersconnect.com, and has won several awards for her poetry. She is currently a business consultant, certified teacher, and a Nationally-Certified Manager of Program Improvement.

Titles by E.A. James:

Spiritual Cosmetics for the Soul (devotionals)
The Last Visitor (historical fiction)
Being a Well Body of Believers (nonfiction)
This Hill I Climb (poetry)
The Reason Why I Sing (poetry/songs)
Driving Tips for BOOHs (Bats Out of Hell) (satire)
7-Day Emergency Help for OWIACs (Of Whom I Am Chief) (devotionals)
Why I Should Hate Men, But Don't (nonfiction)
Will Work for Food, Family & Freedom (nonfiction)
Casino Con: An Eye-Opening Look From the Inside Out (nonfiction)

Book Ordering Information

To order other books by E.A. James or books published by FM Publishing Company, or to inquire about screenplay production rights, go to:

www.fmpublishingcompany.com

www.blackbusinessnetwork.com/doctorlj

www.createspace.com

www.amazon.com

www.lightningsource.com

Email: fmpublishing@cox.net

Fax: 800-518-1219

www.ingramcontent.com/pod-product-compliance
Lightning Source LLC
Chambersburg PA
CBHW060041050426
42448CB00012B/3096